The Berenstain Bears®
LEARN ABOUT
COLORS

Stan & Jan Berenstain

Westport, Connecticut

Red! Red!
We love red!

The color of a barn
painted barn red.
The bright, bright red
of a woodpecker's head.

Yellow! Yellow!
We love yellow!

The color of the sun,
of the sun's bright beam.
The yummy color
of lemon ice cream.

Do we love blue?
You bet we do!

The color of the sky?
Yes! Yes! Yes!
The color of Mama Bear's
polka-dot dress!

We love colors—
red, yellow, and blue!
Hooray for yellow,
red, and blue!

But there are
other colors, too.

They *come from*
yellow, red, and blue.

Mixing colors
is lots of fun.
Come, we'll show you
how it's done.

Mix red and yellow,
and what do you get?

Orange! Orange
is what you get!

The color of a leaf
about to drop.
The color of a farmer's
pumpkin crop.

The color of his carrot.

The color of his hat.

The color of his

orange-colored cat.

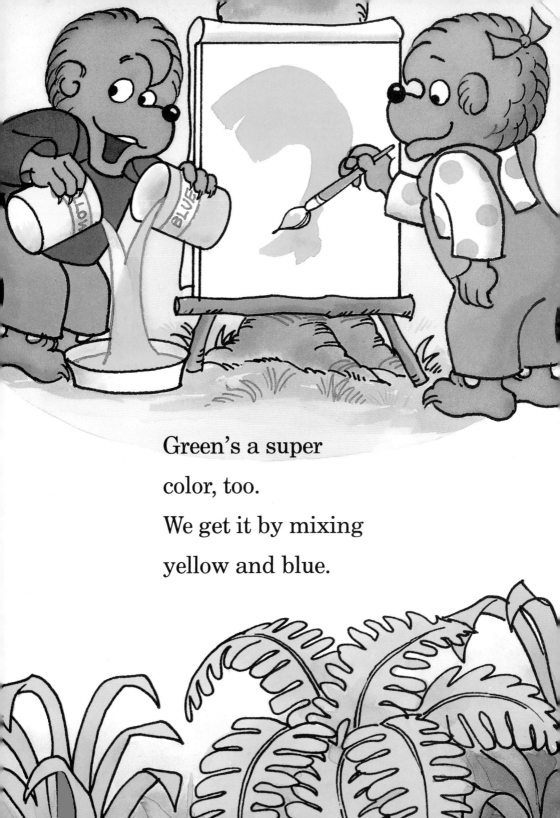

Green's a super
color, too.
We get it by mixing
yellow and blue.

Just between
us bears and you,
it's nature's
favorite color, too!

Though all greens
share a single name,
all greens, dear friends,
are not the same.

Some are dark.

Some are light.

Some are dull.

Some are bright.

This fact, friends,
is also true
of all the other
colors, too.

Colors! Colors!
Dull and bright!
We love colors,
dark and light!

Wait! What about purple,
which, don't forget,
is also known
as violet?

We get purple,
rich and fine,
when red and blue
we do combine.

It's the color of grapes
on the vine.
The color of the feet
that make the wine.

We love yellow,
red, and blue.
We love green
and orange, too.
And purple, of course,
which, don't forget,
is also known
as violet.

We see those colors
and lots more
at the paint
and hardware store!

Beige and tan,
buff and brown—
the colors of the bears
in our town!

We love the color
of every bear!

The colors of the clothes
that they wear!

The sunset colors
at the end of day!

At night the colors
all fade away.

It grows dark,
and darker still.

Will the colors come back...?

Yes! Yes!

Yes, they will!

It's the dawn
of another day!
The sun comes up!
Hooray! Hooray!
We get up,
go out, and say—

We love colors,
red, yellow, and blue!
We love green
and orange, too!
And purple, of course,
which, don't forget,
is also known as violet!